How to use this book

Follow the advice, in italics, given for you on each page.
Praise *the children at every step!*

Detailed guidance is provided in the Read Write Inc. Phonics Handbook.

7 reading activities

Children:

☆ *Practise reading the speed sounds.*

☆ *Read the green and red words for the Ditty.*

☆ *Listen as you read the introduction.*

☆ *Read the Ditty.*

☆ *Re-read the Ditty and discuss the 'questions to talk about'.*

☆ *Re-read the Ditty with fluency and expression.*

☆ *Practise reading the speed words.*

Speed Sounds

Consonants

Say the pure sounds (do not add 'uh').

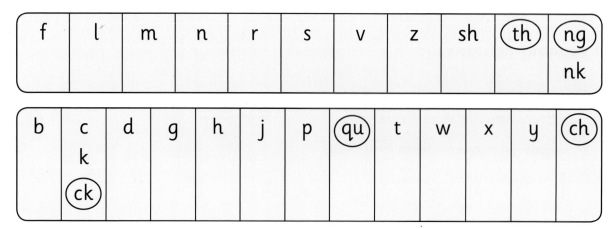

f	l	m	n	r	s	v	z	sh	th	ng
										nk

b	c	d	g	h	j	p	qu	t	w	x	y	ch
	k											
	ck											

Vowels

Say the sounds in and out of order.

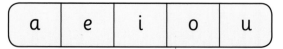

a	e	i	o	u

Each box contains only one sound. Focus sounds are circled.

Ditty 1 # Let's sing

Green words

Read in Fred Talk (pure sounds).

can   dog   frog   si<u>ng</u>

<u>ch</u>i<u>ck</u>   du<u>ck</u>   so<u>ng</u>   a

Read the root word first and then with the ending.

let → let's

Red words

<u>the</u>

Ditty 1 # Let's sing

Introduction

Do you like singing? In this story lots of animals have fun singing.

the frog can sing

the du<u>ck</u> can si<u>ng</u>

the <u>th</u>e dog can si<u>ng</u>

the chick can sing

let's sing a song

Ditty 2 # Kiss Kiss

Green words

Read in Fred Talk (pure sounds).

cot   kiss   rug   with   duck

bath   in   quack   on   his

Red words

the

Ditty 2 # Kiss kiss

Introduction

Do you have a younger brother or sister? In this story we meet a baby.
Let's see what he likes doing.

on <u>the</u> rug

ma-ma

in <u>the</u> ba<u>th</u> wi<u>th</u> his du<u>ck</u>

<u>qu</u>a<u>ck</u> <u>qu</u>a<u>ck</u>

in his cot

ki<u>ss</u> ki<u>ss</u>

Ditty 3 # La-la-la

Green words

Read in Fred Talk (pure sounds).

can   ba**ng**   drum   si**ng**
wi**th**   band

Read the root word first and then with the ending.

lot → lots   so**ng** → so**ng**s

Red words

I   **th**e   of

Ditty 3 La-la-la

Introduction
Do you play a musical instrument? This is a story about a girl who really likes music.

I can bang the drum

bang bang

12

I can sing lots of songs

la-la-la

I can sing with the band

Questions to talk about

Ditty 1

Which animal sings first?

What do the animals do at the end of the story?

What song shall we sing?

Ditty 2

What does the baby have with him in the bath?

What does Mum do before the baby goes to sleep?

What do you like doing at bathtime/bedtime?

Ditty 3

What instrument can the girl play?

What does the girl do in the band?

What musical instrument would you like to play in a band?

Speed words for Ditty 1

Children practise reading the words across the rows, down the columns and in and out of order clearly and quickly.

can	dog	frog	sing
chick	duck	song	a

Speed words for Ditty 2

cot	on	kiss	the
duck	with	bath	in

Speed words for Ditty 3

can	I	bang	drum
song	with	of	sing